Day by Day Through the Easter Season

Reverend Mark G. Boyer

LIGUORI
PUBLICATIONS

One Liguori Drive
Liguori, Missouri 63057
(314) 464-2500

Imprimi Potest:
Stephen T. Palmer, C.SS.R.
Provincial, St. Louis Province
Redemptorist Fathers

Imprimatur:
+ Edward J. O'Donnell
Vicar General, Archdiocese of St. Louis

ISBN 0-89243-278-0
Library of Congress Catalog Card Number: 87-82945

Dedicated to
Arthur Lee Hobbs
who continues to be a friend
on the journey.

TABLE OF CONTENTS

Sixth Sunday of Easter

Seventh Sunday of Easter

Solemnity of Pentecost

FOREWORD

The Easter Season consists of a fifty-day celebration beginning with the Easter Vigil and ending with Pentecost Sunday. During these days the Scripture themes focus on the abundance of new life brought about by the Resurrection of Jesus from the dead. The first week of Easter features the reactions of those who encounter resurrected life for the first time. The second week outlines the themes of birth, wind, and light. Food and drink are highlighted during the third week, while sheep, shepherds, and sheepfolds are featured during the fourth week. The focal points of the fifth week are vines, branches, peace, and friends. The twin themes of departure and the promise of the Spirit highlight the sixth week, while the seventh week prepares for the fulfillment of the promise of the gift of the Spirit on Pentecost.

Many people scrupulously observe Lent but seem to ignore Easter, which, after all, is the reason for Lenten preparation. This book is meant to help people observe Easter and to help them to celebrate and to bask in the new life that has taken place in their lives. It is hoped that these pages will be of some help in keeping all fifty days of the Easter Season alive!

The exercise for each day is divided into four parts. (1) A selection from Scripture has been chosen from the Gospel assigned for the day. (2) A reflection expands some aspect of the Scripture in relationship to the eternal life theme of the season. (3) A reaction question is provided for readers in order to direct their thoughts. Hopefully, this contemplation will lead readers to practical application of the Scripture in their lives and enable them to see how the Word of God is already alive there. (4) A prayer attempts to link the Scripture reading and the reflection to the personal application.

This book is meant as a tool to help people respond to the Word of God and to celebrate the new life that he has given everyone. It is the author's wish that an awareness of this abundant life course through every person during the whole fifty days of Easter.

Mark G. Boyer

NOTE: Cycle A: 1990, 1993, 1996, etc.
           Cycle B: 1988, 1991, 1994, etc.
           Cycle C: 1989, 1992, 1995, etc.

EASTER SUNDAY

Cycles A, B, and C
An Open Tomb

On the first day of the week, Mary of Magdala came to the tomb early in the morning, while it was still dark, and saw the stone removed from the tomb. So she ran and went to Simon Peter and to the other disciple whom Jesus loved, and told them, "They have taken the Lord from the tomb, and we don't know where they put him." So Peter and the other disciple went out and came to the tomb (John 20:1-3).

Reflection: Ordinarily people do not like to be near a tomb in the depth of night. There is something scary and frightening about being alone in a dark cemetery. If this is not enough, finding the tomb open would make most people panic and run away. And the story they tell makes others run toward the spot to see for themselves.

So often it is the tomb of people's lives that is found to have had its entrance stone rolled away. At first, such an event is frightening to the individual person and others. But curiosity almost always prevails and others run toward it, hoping to see the new life that seems to emerge from empty tombs.

Reaction: What tomb of your life has had its entrance stone rolled away so that a new approach to life began to emerge?

Prayer: God of the early morning, in the beginning, after you created the sixth day, you molded people from the clay of the earth and gave them the breath of life. Likewise, on the first day of your new creation your Spirit stirred up life in the tomb where your Son slept in death. From the tombs of our lives roll away the entrance stone which keeps us from total openness with you. Bring us to the light of the resurrection with Jesus, who with you and the Holy Spirit are one God, for ever and ever. Amen.

MONDAY
Fear and Joy

They [Mary Magdalene and the other Mary] went away quickly from the tomb, fearful yet overjoyed, and ran to announce this to his disciples. And behold, Jesus met them on their way and greeted them. They approached, embraced his feet, and did him homage. Then Jesus said to them, "Do not be afraid. Go tell my brothers to go to Galilee, and there they will see me" (Matthew 28:8-10).

Reflection: The experience of new life leaves everyone fearful and joyful. People feel fear because it is hard to believe that there really is life after suffering through a problem, an illness, or some other crisis situation. They sense joy because they know that because of the suffering they are now much more human. In this moment of suspension between fear and joy, Jesus usually appears in a person, a gift, the song of a bird, or the serenity of a quiet place. These people find themselves engaged in a second of worship, which is followed by an inner compulsion to go and share the experience with others. They hope that others will see what they themselves have witnessed.

Reaction: When was the last time you experienced the Lord in your life? Did you feel fear and joy at the same time?

Prayer: God of fear and joy, when you reveal yourself to your people, the whole earth bows down in worship; the winds whisper your message; the rivers sing your praise; and the sun illuminates the work of your hands. As we hurry on our way today, come and meet us in those others we greet. Together may all of us share the experience of the presence of the resurrected Jesus, who with you and the Holy Spirit are one God, for ever and ever. Amen.

TUESDAY
Weeping

Mary [of Magdala] stayed outside the tomb weeping. And as she wept, she bent over into the tomb. . . . She turned around and saw Jesus there, but did not know it

was Jesus. . . . Jesus said to her, "Mary!" She turned
and said to him in Hebrew, "Rabbouni," which means
Teacher (John 20:11,14,16).

Reflection: How often do people weep over the past instead of
turning to face the future? They curiously peer into the depths of
the past, conjuring up as much sorrow as possible for the
fleeting quality of all life. Weeping becomes an outward sign of
hopelessness. Those who mourn need a teacher, one who will
revive in them a hope for the future; one who will promise that
life exists not in the past but in a new and changed state in the
present and on into the future. Such teachers often appear out of
nowhere and once they have done their job disappear just as
quickly. It is of the utmost importance that the teacher address
the student by name. One who weeps needs to be called by name
out of the weeping for the past to the joy of the present encounter
with life.

Reaction: When was the last time that you found yourself
weeping over the past? Did your weeping help you to face the
future?

Prayer: God of all who weep, by name you called your Son,
Jesus, out of the tomb of sorrow to the joy of the Resurrection.
Through Baptism you have called us by name out of the waters
of death to the streams of new life. When we are weeping for the
past, send us teachers who, like Jesus, will guide us through the
Paschal Mystery to the hope of sharing in eternal life with you,
Jesus, and the Holy Spirit, one God, for ever and ever. Amen.

WEDNESDAY
Sharing Life

It happened that, while he [Jesus] was with them [two of his disciples] at table, he took bread, said the blessing, broke it, and gave it to them. With that their eyes were opened and they recognized him, but he vanished from their sight (Luke 24:30-31).

Reflection: Eating meals with others is a very important activity. When people share food together they also share their lives with each other. Just as people hunger for bread as physical nourishment, so they likewise hunger for relationships as social nourishment. All persons are social by nature and have a corresponding hunger for others. Such social hunger often goes unnamed and the nonsatisfied individual may attempt to solve the problem by overeating or overdrinking. When people share themselves with each other in relationships, they form a support system for each other, and they create a spirit that opens their eyes so they can recognize their needs. Once human needs are recognized, they can be satisfied by the mutual sharing of the persons concerned.

Reaction: Make a list of at least three persons who "feed" you. What "food" does each person share with you?

Prayer: God of the hungry, you fed your Chosen People with manna during their forty years in the desert, and you nourished your servant Elijah with food for his forty-day journey to your holy mountain. Jesus, your Son, not only broke bread with his friends but he gave himself as food to them as well. Make our relationships with others feed us with new life. Enable us to offer others the bread of truth. And guide all people to the banquet of heaven where their eyes will be opened and they will recognize you, your Son, and your Holy Spirit as the one God, who lives and reigns for ever and ever. Amen.

THURSDAY
Truth

While they [the disciples of Jesus] were still incredulous for joy and were amazed, he asked them, "Have you anything here to eat?" They gave him a piece of baked fish; he took it and ate it in front of them (Luke 24:41-43).

Reflection: At times it is difficult to admit or to accept the truth. Some people even pretend that the truth is not really the truth, but they deceive themselves. "It can't be true that John is dead; he was alive just yesterday!" "It can't be true that Evelyn said that about me; she has always been one of my best friends!" "It can't be true that the Smiths are divorcing; they've been together for thirty years!" "It can't be true that I won all this money; I never win anything!" Truth is difficult to grasp at times, but the eating of fish is easy for the senses to grasp. Given the time to chew on it, truth becomes easier to admit, to accept, and, finally, to swallow in the presence of others. Joy and wonder fade, and the reality of the true situation is comprehended.

Reaction: Have you ever been faced with a truth you found almost impossible to believe? If so, why did you find it so difficult?

Prayer: God of eternal verity, you reveal your truth to people of every time and place. Your servant Moses spoke your word of freedom to your people. When your people sinned, your prophets spoke your forgiveness to them. In Jesus of Nazareth, your truth took flesh as he unveiled resurrected life. Give us a share in this life and fill us with joy and wonder at the meal of your presence with Jesus, your Son, and with the Holy Spirit, who with you are one God, for ever and ever. Amen.

FRIDAY
Telling Others What to Do

Jesus revealed himself again to his disciples at the Sea of Tiberias. He revealed himself in this way. . . . When it was already dawn, Jesus was standing on the shore; but the disciples did not realize that it was Jesus. Jesus said to them, "Children, have you caught anything to eat?" They answered him, "No." So he said to them, "Cast the net over the right side of the boat and you will find something." So they cast it, and were not able to pull it in because of the number of fish (John 21:1,4-6).

Reflection: So often we see people standing at the shores of others' lives telling them what to do. Usually, they begin by asking, "Do you know what you are doing?" More often than not, the answer is, "Why don't you mind your own business? I know what I'm doing!" Some persons will continue their actions — to the point of starvation — even if they don't know what they are doing! It is presupposed that those standing on the shore of others' lives do not know any more than the distraught fishermen described in John's Gospel. But that presupposition is wrong. Those who are unbuffeted by the sea may be able to see better than the fishermen themselves; they may have been in the same situation before, and they do know what they are doing. It is good that those on shore are solicitous for those at sea; otherwise, these latter might either drown or starve to death when the fish are simply on the other side!

Reaction: How did you react to others who told you what to do when they actually did know more about it than you? How would you respond to such a person now?

Prayer: God of wisdom, once you directed a few of your people through the flood to a new creation. Later, when your people were oppressed, you led them through the Sea of Reeds to freedom. You have led us through the baptismal waters of death to the fullness of life in your Spirit. Do not let us drown in the depths of our stubbornness and our limited concerns. Send us someone at daybreak to stand on our shores and point out a new way. Fill our nets with the resurrected life which you share with Jesus, your Son, and the Holy Spirit, who live and reign with you as one God, for ever and ever. Amen.

SATURDAY
Getting Started

He [Jesus] said to them [the disciples]: ''Go into the whole world and proclaim the gospel to every creature'' (Mark 16:15).

Reflection: How difficult it is for most people to get started on a project! The right tools have to be gathered. The right equipment is needed. Sufficient help must be ensured. Then, once everything is ready, the individual person has to be motivated to begin. Procrastination seems to be the easier way! No wonder the proclamation of the good news that Jesus is alive takes so long to be heard. The message cannot be delivered unless those entrusted with it first of all begin.

Reaction: When was the last time that you proclaimed the good news of the Resurrection of Jesus?

Prayer: God of the universe, you have never ceased to reveal the beauty of your face to the whole world. In the past you sent messages to your Chosen People through your prophets. In the fullness of time, your Word became flesh in Jesus of Nazareth. He proclaimed the good news of your reign, and has entrusted to us this message. Prompt us with your Holy Spirit so that we may make you known throughout the world. We ask this through our Lord Jesus Christ, the risen One, who lives and reigns with you and the Holy Spirit, one God, for ever and ever. Amen.

SECOND SUNDAY OF EASTER

Cycles A, B, and C
Locked Doors

On the evening of that first day of the week, when the doors were locked, where the disciples were, for fear of the Jews, Jesus came and stood in their midst and said to them, "Peace be with you." When he had said this, he showed them his hands and his side. The disciples rejoiced when they saw the Lord. [Jesus] said to them again, "Peace be with you" (John 20:19-21).

Reflection: All people have locked doors behind which lies an inner, secret place that only they inhabit. Behind that locked door there exists the fullness of life. However, fear keeps a person not only from opening it but may cause an individual to add an additional dead bolt to the ones already in place there. But fear disables; it acts as a deterrent to opening locked doors and sharing in new life. Confronted with such a locked door a person needs someone, a confidante, a trusted friend, who can pass through the door and eliminate the fear so that the new life on the other side can walk through. Unless that door is penetrated, fear will cause the life that exists on the other side to wither.

Reaction: Are there any locked doors of fear that exist in your life?

Prayer: God of peace, your presence in the world often goes undetected. You pass through the locked doors that fear erects, and you call forth the life that exists on the other side just like you called forth your Son, Jesus Christ, from the sealed tomb. Penetrate the locked doors of our minds and our hearts, remove our fears, inspire us to rejoice at the sight of new life, and bring us into the peace of your kingdom, where you live with Jesus and the Holy Spirit, one God, for ever and ever. Amen.

(Alternative Selection)
Sharing Experiences

Thomas, called Didymus, one of the Twelve, was not with them when Jesus came. . . . Now a week later his disciples were again inside and Thomas was with them. Jesus came, although the doors were locked, and stood in their midst and said, "Peace be with you." Then he said to Thomas, "Put your finger here and see my hands, and bring your hand and put it into my side, and do not be

unbelieving, but believe." Thomas answered and said to him, "My Lord and my God!" (John 20:24,26-28)

Reflection: How often have people, who missed an experience that many others have shared, been shattered by the reaction of those who witnessed the event. Nothing can replace the experience. Those who do not participate in the event cannot understand the enthusiasm of those who do. Those who do not participate have their doubts and refuse to believe that something could be as magnificent as those who experienced it continue to insist. It is only after those doubters have an opportunity to witness what the others have witnessed that they can understand the belief shared by the group that first experienced it. Once this is accomplished all stand on common ground, understand each other, and celebrate the new life brought into existence by the event.

Reaction: Have you ever tried to relate a magnificent experience from your life to someone who has not had the same or similar experience? What were the results?

Prayer: God of doubters, you never cease to lead your people through the experiences of doubts to the moments of faith. Even though your people failed to believe in you, you never abandoned them. Rather, you promised to be with them. Be with us as our twin when we do not believe. Lead us through the experiences of this life to the moment of eternal life. We ask this through our Lord Jesus Christ, your Son, who lives and reigns with you and the Holy Spirit, one God, for ever and ever. Amen.

MONDAY
Born Again

Jesus answered and said to him [Nicodemus], "Amen, amen, I say to you, no one can see the kingdom of God without being born from above." Nicodemus said to him, "How can a person once grown old be born again? Surely he cannot reenter his mother's womb and be born again, can he?" Jesus answered, "Amen, amen, I say to you, no one can enter the kingdom of God without being born of water and Spirit. What is born of flesh is flesh and what is born of spirit is spirit" (John 3:3-6).

Reflection: The birth of a child is an event that causes both men and women to stand back in wonder. The child did not ask to be born. Furthermore, the baby is forced from the comfortable warmth of the mother's womb and bathed, clothed, fed, and placed in a foreign world of lights, blankets, and strange voices. No human person would ever want to repeat such a traumatic experience as birth! Nevertheless, the child discovers that authentic life is found only in repeatedly being born again. Plunged into the wet tomb of Baptism, the child rises to a new birth of water and Spirit. Plunged into early life, the youngster rises to a new birth of exploring the surrounding world. Plunged into school, the student rises to a new birth of learning. Plunged into adolescence, the teenager rises to a new birth of uniqueness. The plunges continue through college, vocation, mid-life, retirement, and so on. And with each plunge there also comes a new birth. The final plunge is into death; the final birth is to eternal life. Every plunge is an experience of the kingdom of God!

Reaction: How many times have you been born again?

Prayer: God of birth, long ago you promised the childless couple, Abraham and Sarah, that they would have a child and that their descendants would be as numerous as the sands on the shore of the sea. Keeping your promise, Sarah gave birth to Israel, whose twelve sons became the tribes of your Chosen People. From these people you chose Mary, who gave birth to your own Son, Jesus. By his example, he taught us the necessity of being reborn throughout our lives. From the womb of death he was born again to a new life. Plunge us into the mystery of his life and death, and bring us to new birth in him, who with you and the Holy Spirit are one God, for ever and ever. Amen.

TUESDAY
Wind

"The wind blows where it wills, and you can hear the sound it makes, but you do not know where it comes from or where it goes; so it is with everyone who is born of the Spirit" (John 3:8).

Reflection: The hand of the breeze grasps the wind catcher and rattles the chimes producing deep melodious sounds. The draft cannot be seen, but it can be heard! The breeze cannot be seen, but it rustles the leaves on the trees. The wind cannot be held, but it is felt on faces, arms, and legs. No one knows from whence it comes or to where it goes; the wind is free. To experience the wind is to experience birth by the Spirit into the freedom of God. Such a birth in the wind-swept Spirit inspires people to let God breathe new life into them.

Reaction: What new life is God breathing into you?

Prayer: God of the four winds, at creation a mighty wind swept over the formlessness of the earth and brought forth abundant life. Into humankind you breathed the breath of your Spirit and set all people free. Even while your Son slept in the tomb of death, a gentle breeze awakened him to the fullness of freedom — eternal life. Send your breeze to rustle our lives and waken us to the freedom of our resurrection. We ask this through our Lord Jesus Christ, your Son, who lives and reigns with you and the Holy Spirit, one God, for ever and ever. Amen.

WEDNESDAY
Light

"The light came into the world, but people preferred darkness to light, because their works were evil. For everyone who does wicked things hates the light and does not come toward the light, so that his works might not be

exposed. But whoever lives the truth comes to the light, so that his works may be clearly seen as done in God" (John 3:19-21).

Reflection: Light is always coming into the world. Someone has a question; another person has the answer: Light has come into the world. One person has a problem; another person is willing to listen: Light has come into the world. Two people are deadlocked in the midst of negotiations; a third individual offers an entirely different solution acceptable to both negotiators: Light has come into the world. It is only when there is no one to give an answer, when there is no one to listen, when there is no one willing to propose another solution that darkness reigns. The stubbornness of those unwilling to admit that they do not possess the whole truth discloses how much some people prefer darkness. Darkness covers human limitations. Light reveals how equal in dignity all people are and how much they need each other for the sharing of light.

Reaction: Who has been light for you most recently? How did that person illuminate your darkness?

Prayer: God of light, you created the sun to shine on us during the day and the moon to illumine the night. You led your Chosen People from slavery to freedom with a column of cloud by day and a column of fire by night. Through your prophets you brightened your people with your word of truth. Continue to scatter the darkness of our hearts and minds. Through Jesus, your Son, guide us to the eternal light, where you live and reign with him and the Holy Spirit, one God, for ever and ever. Amen.

THURSDAY
Words of God

"For the one whom God sent speaks the words of God. He does not ration his gift of the Spirit. The Father loves the Son and has given everything over to him. Whoever believes in the Son has eternal life, but whoever disobeys the Son will not see life" (John 3:34-36).

Reflection: How difficult it is to speak the words of God! Most people prefer to speak their own words. One person begins every sentence with "I." Another individual pompously declares that he knows what ought to be done in every situation. Other persons are the sole authority on any given topic. All of these people speak their own words, and more often than not what they say sounds old, worn out, lifeless. However, the person whom God sends speaks the words of God which are new, fresh, and filled with life. The way to determine the manner in which individuals are speaking is to listen and judge whether or not their speech stirs up life in the hearers. Those who speak life are the ones sent from God.

Reaction: Recall a time when someone's words stirred up life in you. Did you consider this person a gift from God?

Prayer: God of speech, from the beginning of time you spoke words of earth, sea, sky, sun, moon, trees, fish, cattle, man and woman. Your words had life and created reality. Throughout time you have continued to speak to the work of your hands. Jesus, your Son, became your incarnate Word. He revealed the

limitlessness of your words of life. Help us to listen attentively
to those who speak your words of truth, so that we might share
in the eternal love of your Son and your Spirit, who with you live
and reign as one God, for ever and ever. Amen.

FRIDAY
Meager Resources

**One of his disciples, Andrew, the brother of Simon Peter,
said to him, "There is a boy here who has five barley
loaves and two fish; but what good are these for so
many?" . . . Then Jesus took the loaves, gave thanks,
and distributed them to those who were reclining, and
also as much of the fish as they wanted (John 6:8-9,11).**

Reflection: It is amazing how the resources always seem to be
so meager in the midst of the vast needs of so many. What is so
often forgotten, however, is that less is more and more is less.
Such an insight makes no sense to a capitalistic mind. The truth
is illumined when one person shares nothing but a cup of coffee
with another; it is surprising how just a cup of coffee refreshes
one.

Someone unexpectedly stops by for a visit: "Have you had
lunch yet? Would you like to have a bowl of soup with me?"
The bowl of soup amazingly satisfies hunger. Take a crumb of
bread and a sip of wine and suddenly a crowd is nourished. Less
is more and more is less; little revelations each day confirm this
truth. The response to a cup of coffee, a bowl of soup, a bite of

bread, a sip of wine, or five barley loaves and two fish is one of thanksgiving. There is no need to hoard meager resources; by sharing them they multiply and can satisfy many needs.

Reaction: Recall a situation in your life when you shared from the little you had and watched it multiply before your eyes.

Prayer: God of the meager, when your Chosen People were thirsty, you brought forth water from the rock. When they were without meat, you sent them quail. And when they hungered for bread, you rained down manna from heaven. From the little of life you create abundance. Move us to share the meager resources of our lives, our country, and our world, so that the needs of many may be satisfied. Enable us to give thanks to you for all your gifts and to share in the fullness of life with Jesus, your Son, and the Holy Spirit, who lives and reigns with you, one God, for ever and ever. Amen.

SATURDAY
Rough Sea

The sea was stirred up because a strong wind was blowing. When they [the disciples] had rowed about three or four miles, they saw Jesus walking on the sea and coming near the boat, and they began to be afraid. But he said to them, "It is I. Do not be afraid." They wanted to take him into the boat, but the boat immediately arrived at the shore to which they were heading (John 6:18-21).

Reflection: Whenever the sea of the world begins to be stirred by the winds of change and individual lifeboats begin to be tossed about, people respond with fear. They prefer calm seas, light breezes, and little list in their lives. Fear is the first reaction to the opposite of these because what is known and comfortable is headed toward what is unknown and disturbing. "Don't rock the boat!" Such status quo existence, however, is deadly; there is no life without wind and surf. It is only by facing the rough sea and holding onto the boat that life can ever be experienced in its fullness. And once the stormy crisis is over, in retrospect it is seen that the situation was not so bad after all; for the boat has arrived at the shore, which was actually nearby. Those in the boat usually realize — sooner or later — that there was no reason to be afraid because the Lord was with them all along.

Reaction: How do you react to the rough seas of life?

Prayer: God of the water, through the turbulence of slavery you led your Chosen People to the shores of freedom. Out of the sea of death you brought your Son safely to the shore of eternal life. Be with us always. Guide us through the storms of our lives to the shores of the fullness of resurrected life. We ask this through our Lord Jesus Christ, who lives and reigns with you and the Holy Spirit, one God, for ever and ever. Amen.

THIRD SUNDAY OF EASTER

Cycle A
Pilgrimage of Life

Now that very day two of them were going to a village seven miles from Jerusalem called Emmaus, and they were conversing about all the things that had occurred. And it happened that while they were conversing and debating, Jesus himself drew near and walked with them (Luke 24:13-15).

Reflection: The pilgrimage that is named life consists of a ceaseless journey from one place to another. So often people are dissatisfied with where they are, and they long to be elsewhere. This restlessness is observed in society's mobility, in the ability to flip from one television station to another searching for entertainment, and in the busy activity that forms everyday scheduled existence. What is often omitted in the journey is the discussion. Only in the exchange of ideas can something new be born. A lively exchange between people can produce insights that cannot be gleaned alone and that would have otherwise been lost forever.

Reaction: Name a person with whom you recently had a discussion and discovered something new. What was your discussion about? What new insight did you discover?

Prayer: God of the journey, you led your Chosen People out of Egyptian slavery through the waters of the Sea of Reeds to the Promised Land of freedom. In Jesus, your Son, you pitched your tent among us and continue to travel with us on our pilgrim way. The fire of the light of Christ given to us in Baptism lights the way for us to a new city named heaven. Guide our steps, inspire our sharing, move us to conversion, and help us to recognize the presence of Christ with us on our pilgrimage to you, who live with Jesus and the Holy Spirit as one God, for ever and ever. Amen.

Cycle B
Repeated Experiences

Then the two [disciples] recounted what had taken place on the way [to Emmaus] and how he [Jesus] was made known to them in the breaking of the bread.

While they were still speaking about this, he stood in their midst and said to them, "Peace be with you." But they were startled and terrified and thought that they were seeing a ghost (Luke 24:35-37).

Reflection: It is important that experiences be repeated in order to confirm and verify them. When people gather together to celebrate the Eucharist on occasion, they may tell others that they had a moving experience: "This was a beautiful Mass." "The music was special today." "Everyone really seemed to be a part of what was happening." In other words, they encountered Jesus in the breaking of the bread. But this one encounter is not enough. Next week the experience needs to be repeated; it needs confirmation and verification. They must return to Jerusalem. Otherwise, people may begin to doubt resurrected life and believe in ghosts. It is more convenient to believe in ghosts than to live real life!

Reaction: When was the last time that you experienced Jesus in the breaking of the bread in an unusual way? What made this such a memorable experience?

Prayer: God of authentic life, you reveal yourself as the God of the living. When your Son, Jesus, was put to death, you raised him to new life. Strengthen our faith in his Resurrection and help us to recognize him in the breaking of the bread. We ask this through the same Jesus Christ, who lives and reigns with you and the Holy Spirit, one God, for ever and ever. Amen.

Cycle C: (Long Form)
Trust

Jesus said to Simon Peter, "Simon, son of John, do you love me more than these?" He said to him, "Yes, Lord, you know that I love you." He said to him, "Feed my

lambs." He then said to him a second time, "Simon, son of John, do you love me?" He said to him, "Yes, Lord, you know that I love you." He said to him, "Tend my sheep." He said to him the third time, "Simon, son of John, do you love me?" Peter was distressed that he had said to him a third time, "Do you love me?" and he said to him, "Lord, you know everything; you know that I love you." [Jesus] said to him, "Feed my sheep" (John 21:15-17).

Reflection: Once a person has broken trust with another individual through the telling of a lie, or by stealing, betrayal, whatever, it takes a long time before trust can be restored to the relationship. Authentic love is founded on trust, and it has a need for a response, especially after trust has been broken. This surety gained from response may be grounded in a trinity of love questions, which to the answerer is distressing. The one who loves wants to be sure that a repeat performance of broken trust is not part of the schedule. Love implies that there is ample room for others in the relationship so that love can be shared.

Reaction: Have you ever broken the trust of another? What did it take to restore a loving trust?

Prayer: God of love, even when your people broke trust with you by sin, you never abandoned them. Time after time your people broke your covenant, but you welcomed them back with open arms of love. Through the death and Resurrection of Jesus you demonstrated how much you love us. You already know how much we love you. Strengthen our trust and continue to share with us the triune love of your Son and your Spirit, who with you are one God, for ever and ever. Amen.

Cycle C: (Short Form)
Labor

When they [the disciples] climbed out on shore, they saw a charcoal fire with fish on it and bread. Jesus said to them, "Bring some of the fish you just caught. . . ." Jesus came over and took the bread and gave it to them, and in like manner the fish (John 21:9-10,13).

Reflection: Sooner or later all people learn the joy of eating the fruit of their own labor. Catching only a few fish and preparing them over an open fire provides a sense of self-support. Likewise, there is something special about tilling the soil, planting the grains of wheat, cultivating the young plants, observing them produce fruit, harvesting the produce, and being nourished by the bread of the labor of one's hands. The mystery in the catch and the harvest cannot be lost sight of. Why do the fish bite the bait? Why does the seed sprout, grow, and produce? There is more than just the work of one's hands involved in all of this. The Creator provides the means for people to be joyous in eating the fruit of the labor of their hands. In the eating of the fish and the breaking of the bread there is recognized the One who gives newness to life.

Reaction: Can you point to the fruit of your labor that enabled you to recognize God?

Prayer: God of the sea and field, out of your bounty we make the catch and gather in the harvest. So often in the past you fed your people with quail and manna. Today you bless the work of our hands as we toil to provide for our needs. Continue to sustain us with the food of your Son, Jesus, who fulfills your promise of a new and everlasting life. May we share at the eternal banquet with you, your Son, and your Spirit, united with you, the one God, for ever and ever. Amen.

MONDAY
Seeking Information

When they [the crowd who had just witnessed the multiplication of the loaves] found him [Jesus] across the sea they said to him, "Rabbi, when did you get here?" (John 6:25)

Reflection: "What are you doing here?" "How did you get here?" "Why are you here?" These are questions that people often ask each other. They ask them because they seek the presumed and hidden information that the one asked should be able to reveal. Students do this when they raise their hands to ask the teacher a question. It is important for people to know. The one seeking information usually addresses the one who has the power to give it with "Mr.," "Mrs.," "Ms.," "Miss," "Father," or "Rabbi." Once what is sought has been revealed, the questioner moves on to other fields.

Reaction: The last time that you needed information of any kind, whom did you ask? What did you need to know?

Prayer: God of mystery, people have been seeking to know you and believe in you since time began. Moses, your prophet, was able to speak with you face-to-face as you guided him in the care of your people. In Jesus, your Son, you have enabled us to see you as you are and to know you as the Loving One. Be with us as we continue to seek new life through knowledge. And at the end of our earthly journey, enable us to find you, who live and reign with Jesus Christ and the Holy Spirit, one God, for ever and ever. Amen.

TUESDAY
Bread

Jesus said to them [the crowd], "Amen, amen, I say to you, it was not Moses who gave the bread from heaven; my Father gives you the true bread from heaven. For the bread of God is that which comes down from heaven and

gives life to the world." So they said to him, "Sir, give us this bread always." Jesus said to them, "I am the bread of life; whoever comes to me will never hunger, and whoever believes in me will never thirst" (John 6:32-35).

Reflection: There are so many kinds of bread available today. Edible bread may be white or brown, twisted or rolled, baked or frozen. For some people their work is their bread; work feeds them. Others find that a child is bread; the child satisfies a need to have someone to care for. Still others attest that their bread is composed of suffering; their pain is always with them. Bread is the staple of life in so many ways!

Reaction: What is your bread of life?

Prayer: God of bread, you fed your Chosen People with manna in the desert. You have sent us Jesus, the true bread of heaven, who has given life to the world. Give us this bread always. Satisfy our hunger until we are joined with you in the eternal feast of heaven. We ask this through our Lord Jesus Christ, your Son, who lives and reigns with you and the Holy Spirit, one God, for ever and ever. Amen.

WEDNESDAY
Rejection

"Everything that the Father gives me will come to me, and I will not reject anyone who comes to me, because I came down from heaven not to do my own will but the will of the one who sent me. And this is the will of the one who sent me, that I should not lose anything of what he gave me, but that I should raise it [on] the last day" (John 6:37-39).

Reflection: To be rejected by another is extremely depressing. No person wants to be treated in this way and yet it happens to everyone at some time in life. Parents can reject children. A person may reject a stranger. A crowd can reject a leader. When people are rejected, they feel like they are lost. There are some people, however, who greet those in the midst of rejection and raise them up to life. Rejection does not have to be the last day in one's life.

Reaction: If you ever rejected anyone, do you remember why you did it? Recall the last person who rejected you. Why did that person do it?

Prayer: God of the abandoned, when Jesus, your Son, was rejected and put to death, you did not abandon his broken body, but you raised him to life. Send your Spirit to move us to do your will, and raise us on the last day to life with you, your Son, and your Spirit, one God, for ever and ever. Amen.

THURSDAY
Listening

"Everyone who listens to my Father and learns from him comes to me. Not that anyone has seen the Father except the one who is from God; he has seen the Father" (John 6:45-46).

Reflection: There is a distinction between hearing and listening. Hearing takes place when a person's ears receive vibrations which the brain perceives as sounds. Hearing can take place consciously or unconsciously. People hear radios, the honking of horns, and lots of other sounds that are classified as noise. However, most people do not listen to these sounds. When they listen to a bird singing, a thunderclap, or another individual, they focus their attention on what is being heard. Concentration is a definite aspect of listening. Listening brings pleasure to the one engaged in this activity.

Reaction: Make a list of the things that you have heard during the past day. To which of these did you listen?

Prayer: God of sound, you have blessed us with the gift of listening. We are able to hear your voice in the fresh quiet of the dawn, in the songs of birds, in the rustle of wind through the trees, and in the words of people around us. Open our ears to hear your Word spoken through Jesus, your Son, who lives and reigns with you and the Holy Spirit, one God, for ever and ever. Amen.

FRIDAY
Food and Drink

"Amen, amen, I say to you, unless you eat the flesh of the Son of Man and drink his blood, you do not have life within you. Whoever eats my flesh and drinks my blood has eternal life, and I will raise him on the last day. For my flesh is true food, and my blood is true drink" (John 6:53-55).

Reflection: There are two kinds of food and drink: physical and spiritual. Physical food and drink can be seen, touched, and tasted. It is necessary for the sustenance of life; without it people die. Spiritual food and drink is intangible; it is not accessible to the senses. Yet, spiritual food and drink is necessary for the sustenance of eternal life; without it people will not be raised on the last day. More often than not, physical and spiritual nourishment come intertwined. When people share a meal of food and drink together, the result of the work of their hands — something of their flesh and blood — they also share the depths of their spirits. When people gather to celebrate the spiritual, Eucharistic food and drink, true food and drink, they also share a physical meal of food and drink.

Reaction: When was the last time you shared real physical and real spiritual food and drink with someone? Identify the physical food and the spiritual food that you shared.

Prayer: God of food and drink, in the beginning you planted a garden to provide for the physical needs of your creation. Out of the bounty of your hand you fed your people with manna in the desert and gave them drink from the rock. In these last days you have sent Jesus, your Son, the true bread and the true drink. Give us the food for which we hunger and the drink for which we thirst, Jesus Christ, who with you and your Holy Spirit live and reign as one God, for ever and ever. Amen.

SATURDAY
Freedom to Leave

Many of his [Jesus'] disciples who were listening said, "This saying is hard; who can accept it?" . . . Jesus then said to the Twelve, "Do you also want to leave?" Simon Peter answered him, "Master, to whom shall we go? You have the words of eternal life" (John 6:60,67-68).

Reflection: It is difficult for people to exercise their freedom to leave. Observe a few persons gathered for a committee meeting: Everyone knows that the meeting is accomplishing nothing. All those present are squirming in their seats. Yet, not a single person will stand up and leave. Observe a class of graduates gathered to hear a famous commencement speaker: The sound system is not working properly so that the speaker can barely be heard. It is extremely hot in the room. Yet, no one will get up and leave. Observe a congregation gathered for worship: The musician fails to arrive. The presider is not prepared. Few of the other ministers know what they are doing. Yet, not a single person decides to leave. Not exercising one's freedom to leave could mean that there is nowhere else to go — even when the present situation seems intolerable!

Reaction: When was the last time that you found yourself in a situation where you wanted to get up and leave but did not? Why didn't you leave?

Prayer: God of liberty, you created people to serve you in freedom. Many times people found your words hard to believe; and because they could not accept them, they turned away from you. However, you never abandoned them. Be with us now. Give us an understanding heart as we listen to the words of eternal life of your Son, Jesus Christ, who with you and the Holy Spirit are one God, for ever and ever. Amen.

FOURTH SUNDAY OF EASTER

Cycle A
Doors

"I [Jesus] am the gate for the sheep. All who came [before me] are thieves and robbers, but the sheep did not listen to them. I am the gate. Whoever enters through me will be saved, and will come in and go out and find pasture" (John 10:7-9).

Reflection: In the course of a day people pass through many gates or doors. They come and go through the bedroom, bathroom, kitchen, and front doors of their homes. They glide in and out of car doors. They walk through office, business, department, and supermarket entrances. At airports, bus stations, and train depots, persons pass through gates. Gates and doors are so much a part of the daily routine that they often go ignored. People, too, function as gates or doors. Getting to know a person is the door to friendship. Doing a good job for the boss or supervisor at one's place of employment can be the door to advancement. Speaking to another who listens attentively can be the door to healing. Real doors, be they physical or human, enable others to come in and go out to find salvation.

Reaction: Who has functioned as a gate or door for you recently? How did that person do this?

Prayer: God our Shepherd, with your shepherd's staff you guided your Chosen People through the gate of slavery to the promised land of freedom. Through the death and Resurrection of Jesus you have brought us through the gate of sin to the promised land of eternal life. May we who have entered the sheepfold through the waters of Baptism find the fullness of life in your kingdom, where you live and reign with your Son and the Holy Spirit, one God, for ever and ever. Amen.

Cycle B
Laying Down Life

"I am the good shepherd. A good shepherd lays down his life for the sheep. A hired man, who is not a shepherd and whose sheep are not his own, sees a wolf coming and leaves the sheep and runs away, and the wolf catches and scatters them" (John 10:11-12).

Reflection: In contemporary society it is difficult to find people who are willing to give up their lives for others. In a "me first," "what can I get out of this?" "how do I get to the top?" "get out of my way; here I come" world, no one is willing to take the place of another. If the questions "Could you cover for me?" "Could you substitute for me?" "Could you do a favor for me?" are asked, the usual answer is: "I'm sorry, but I can't; I'm only hired for eight hours a day!" When one person is not willing to help shepherd another one, the human community splinters and scatters. Wolves come in varied styles of clothing today.

Reaction: Do you know someone who would be willing to die for you? Why do you think this to be true?

Prayer: God of the flock, you never leave your people unattended. Throughout the journey of our lives you are with us to protect us and gather us together. Jesus, the Good Shepherd, laid down his life for us, and he taught us to do the same for each other. He did not run away from the Cross, but used it as his shepherd's staff to bring us to share in eternal life. Protect us from the wolf who would scatter us. Lead us to the pasture of eternal life with you, your Son, and your Spirit, who live and reign as one God, for ever and ever. Amen.

Cycle C
Voices

"My sheep hear my voice; I know them, and they follow me. I give them eternal life, and they shall never perish" (John 10:27-28).

Reflection: There are many voices that each person hears each day. The voice of the radio announcer is heard. The reporter's voice is heard on the television. Husbands and wives hear each others' voices as well as those of their children. Workers hear the voices of their managers. In the midst of so many voices, how can people tell which one they are really hearing? Those voices which are really heard are followed. If the radio announcer warns of a traffic accident, an alternative route is quickly chosen and followed. If the reporter relates a neighborhood robbery, the doors are checked to be sure that they are locked. If workers do not follow their managers' directions, they are workers no longer. Out of the many voices each day, those that are truly heard are those that are followed.

Reaction: In the past, which voices did you hear and follow? Which voices do you hear and follow today?

Prayer: God of words, you have been heard throughout the ages by kings, prophets, saints, and sinners. In Jesus, your Son, you spoke to us in human words. Help us to hear his voice and to follow him to the eternal life that he has prepared for us. We ask this through the same Jesus Christ, our Lord, who lives and reigns with you and the Holy Spirit, one God, for ever and ever. Amen.

MONDAY
Groups

"I have other sheep that do not belong to this fold. These also I must lead, and they will hear my voice, and there will be one flock, one shepherd" (John 10:16).

Reflection: People in a group have a tendency to be exclusively centered on preserving the group. If someone new moves into a neighborhood where most people know each other, it is almost impossible for the newcomer to enter into the social life of the neighborhood. If a committee has already been formed and one member was not able to attend the first meeting, that person finds it almost impossible to have an equal voice in the proceedings of the next meeting. Dinner groups, or groups of friends or teams of any kind are very reluctant to permit another person into the group. This is tragic because the group thus loses many valuable contributions.

Reaction: Have you ever attempted to join a group which was not interested in a new member? How did you feel?

Prayer: God of unity, you chose a people to be one with you that you might manifest through them your love for all humankind. You confirmed this desire in Jesus who, through his death and Resurrection, gathered all persons into one fold. Take away all that divides and separates us. Enable us to address all men and women as brothers and sisters. May we one day share in the perfect unity of your Trinity: Father, Son, and Holy Spirit, one God, for ever and ever. Amen.

TUESDAY
Suspense

The Jews gathered around him and said to him, "How long are you going to keep us in suspense? If you are the Messiah, tell us plainly." Jesus answered them, "I told you and you do not believe" (John 10:24-25).

Reflection: Most people like some amount of suspense in their lives — that is, up to a point. In a moment or time of suspense, people do not know what to do or what to believe; they are suspended in the midst of an attempt to decide. Sooner or later they want the suspense to come to an end and a decision to be made. "Give me the answer to the math problem." "Tell me what you think." "Did Jackie do that or not?" After a moment or a time of suspense, people want to be told plainly. What is interesting is that after the suspense is eliminated — when they are told plainly — they reply: "That can't be the answer." "You don't really think that, do you?" "I can't believe that Jackie did that." In other words, they refuse to believe.

Reaction: When was the last time that you experienced suspense in your life? How did you act once it was over?

Prayer: God of suspense, you surprised your people by parting the Sea of Reeds and enabling them to pass through it dry-shod. You halted the course of the Jordan as your people entered the Promised Land. Through the waters of Baptism we have passed from an old life of sin to a new and eternal life. We have come to believe that Jesus is the Messiah. Strengthen us so that we can bear witness to this faith. We ask this through Jesus Christ, our Lord, who lives and reigns with you and the Holy Spirit, one God, for ever and ever. Amen.

WEDNESDAY
Condemnation

"Whoever rejects me [Jesus] and does not accept my words has something to judge him: the word that I spoke, it will condemn him on the last day" (John 12:48).

Reflection: People often condemn others. Sometimes they do it verbally; other times they manifest it silently by refusing to associate with a neighbor whose skin is a different color or by avoiding someone at work and refusing to speak with that person. There are many subtle ways to condemn another individual. The underlying presupposition in the condemnation of another is that the one issuing the condemnation is correct and the condemned is wrong. For condemnation to be verified, someone must be right and someone must be wrong. Furthermore, there is one person who is never condemned — the condemner! People never condemn themselves.

Reaction: Have you ever condemned anyone? If so, was your condemnation justified?

Prayer: God of all peoples, you are always ready to show your mercy when people abandon sin and turn toward you. When your Chosen People turned to idolatry, you sent the prophets to remind them of repentance. In the fullness of time you sent us Jesus, who came not to condemn but to save. He spoke your word, and through his death and Resurrection bestowed on us your mercy. Send your Spirit to work a healing process in those who have been condemned by others. We ask this through our Lord Jesus Christ, your Son, who lives and reigns with you and the Holy Spirit, one God, for ever and ever. Amen.

THURSDAY
Equality

"Amen, amen, I [Jesus] say to you, no slave is greater than his master nor any messenger greater than the one who sent him. If you understand this, blessed are you if you do it" (John 13:16-17).

Reflection: That all people are equal is a common misunderstanding in today's world. All people are equal in human dignity; there is no doubt about that. However, not all are equal in talent. The very differences that exist between one person and another, the characteristics which distinguish one individual from another — these are indications that all people are not equal in talent. It is for this very reason that people need each other; one person supplies what another lacks. The ideal is to work together and produce a harmony grounded in equal human dignity that calls forth the gifts of each person for the good of all people. Those who come to understand this find it to be a holy and healthy way to live.

Reaction: What particular talents has God given to you? How do you use these for the good of others?

Prayer: God of dignity, when you create people you bestow upon each of them an equality of dignity combined with a diversity of gifts. In such multiplicity you reveal the unlimited possibilities of yourself. In the Incarnation of Jesus you confirmed human dignity and raised it to the level of divinity. Enable us to appreciate the gifts of each other. Send us your Spirit to unite our diversity into a harmony of praise to you: Father, Son, and Spirit, one God, for ever and ever. Amen.

FRIDAY
A Dwelling Place

"In my Father's house there are many dwelling places. If there were not, would I have told you that I am going to prepare a place for you? And if I go and prepare a place for you, I will come back again and take you to myself, so that where I am you also may be" (John 14:2-3).

Reflection: Looking for a motel room during the summer in a popular vacation area can be an interesting experience — especially when no reservations have been made in advance. Listening to clerk after clerk say, "I'm sorry, but we are all booked up" or observing the "No vacancy" sign can be depressing after a long day on the road. Sooner or later a room might be found, but only after more driving and much searching and some disappointment. There is another way. A reservation can be made in advance. Then, all the weary traveler has to do, once the motel is located, is to check into a room previously prepared.

Reaction: Have you made a reservation for a room with your God?

Prayer: God of many dwelling places, you cannot be contained for you fill the universe with the essence of your presence. Your desire is that your people may live in your house and enjoy seeing your face forever. Jesus, your Son, the way, the truth, and the life, has prepared a place for us in your home. When he comes back again, may he take us to himself so that we can be one with him and you in the Holy Spirit, one God, for ever and ever. Amen.

SATURDAY
Seeing

"Master, show us the Father, and that will be enough for us." Jesus said to him, "Have I been with you for so long a time and you still do not know me, Philip? Whoever has seen me has seen the Father" (John 14:8-9).

Reflection: Do people see what really exists or do they see only what they want to see? Or, to put this another way, do people see things as they are or do they see things as they fancy them to be? Many people see selectively; they wear blinders; they see only the reality that they believe to exist or only the truth that they have created. This is a safe approach to life; it ensures that nothing strange or different will ever enter into one's field of vision. For these people, everything is clearly defined and regarded as nothing more or nothing less than the seer wants it to be.

But some people struggle to look at things as they are. They attempt to get the whole picture, to look beyond or through the ordinary to the inner and hidden beauty of reality. For these kinds of people life is a stimulating adventure; there is constantly something new and different entering into their field of vision. Reality cannot be mastered; it can only be enjoyed in its multiplicity.

Reaction: Do you see things as they are or do you see things as you are? Give an example.

Prayer: God of all reality, in the beginning you implanted in creation the multiple beauty of yourself. Your crowning work was man and woman formed in your own image and likeness. But this was not enough, for you wanted people to be able to see you. So you sent Jesus, your Son, a man like others except for sin. He enabled us to see you. Give us eyes to look into the hidden beauty of everything and every person around us. May we one day have the privilege of standing before you face-to-face and beholding your triune glory: Father, Son, and Holy Spirit, one God, for ever and ever. Amen.

FIFTH SUNDAY OF EASTER

Cycle A
Ways, Truths, Lifestyles

"Master, we do not know where you are going; how can we know the way?" Jesus said to him [Thomas], "I am the way and the truth and the life. No one comes to the Father except through me" (John 14:5-6).

Reflection: There are many ways to live life. Some people prefer the pursuit of learning and knowledge known as academics. Making money, being prosperous, and getting rich is another way. Other people prefer to give service to others in institutional settings or through some form of religious vocation. There are many truths. Economic truth attempts to relate all that affects the standard of living. Historical truth reveals the past. A personal outlook on life and the world is known as philosophical truth. Lawyers support legal truth. There are many ways to live. Some people seek to get ahead at the expense of others. A few choose to live simply; many are forced into poverty. Whatever way and whatever truth and whatever lifestyle a person chooses indicates where that individual is going.

Reaction: Which way have you chosen? Which truth do you live by? Which lifestyle have you selected?

Prayer: God of pilgrimage, while your Chosen People wandered in the desert, you gave them Moses and Joshua to guide their footsteps to the Promised Land flowing with milk and honey. You have sent us Jesus to guide our steps during our journey to you. Make us faithful followers of Jesus, the way, the truth, and the life, who lives and reigns with you and the Holy Spirit, one God, for ever and ever. Amen.

Cycle B
Pruning

"I am the true vine, and my Father is the vine grower. He takes away every branch in me that does not bear fruit, and everyone that does he prunes so that it bears more fruit" (John 15:1-2).

Reflection: Every year after the harvest of grapes is completed and the process of making wine has begun, the vine grower must go through the vineyard and prune the vines. With his tools he clips off most of the year's new growth until all that remains is a gnarled and twisted brown branch. If there is a branch that has not borne fruit, then the entire branch is removed so that a new vine may be planted to grow in its place. It would seem that such yearly cutting back of the vine would ultimately kill it. However, the contrary is true: the pruning of one year ensures the harvest of the following year.

Reaction: In what way have you pruned yourself in order to be fruitful?

Prayer: God of the vine, you created a vineyard of your Chosen People. You planted them and cared for them and pruned them to make them fruitful. From this people you brought forth your Son, Jesus, the true vine. May we who have been grafted onto him learn the mystery of pruning so that we might bear fruit abundantly. We ask this through our Lord Jesus Christ, who lives and reigns with you and the Holy Spirit, one God, for ever and ever. Amen.

Cycle C
Measurements

"I give you a new commandment: love one another. As I have loved you, so you also should love one another. This is how all will know that you are my disciples, if you have love for one another" (John 13:34-35).

Reflection: People are always measuring things. They measure inches, feet, and yards. They measure pints, quarts, and gallons. They measure teaspoons and tablespoons. Long and short, high and low, above and below, and vertical and horizontal are all measurements. How can one measure love? Some people measure love by how they feel; for them the degree of emotional response is the measure of love. Others measure love by the gifts that are exchanged between the parties concerned; the greater the size or value of a gift indicates the amount of love. But the true measure of love lies in how well those who love imitate each other; love is present when people esteem others as they esteem themselves.

Reaction: What do you use as a measure of love?

Prayer: God of love, you have never ceased to care for all that you have created. You love people into existence; you love them throughout their lives; and you love them into the fullness of life with you. Jesus became the incarnation of your love. Out of love he died on the Cross. But while he slept in death, you loved him to Resurrection. Stir in us a greater appreciation of your love for us. Help us to follow the command of Jesus to love one another. Grant that one day we may share in your triune love: Father, Son, and Holy Spirit, one God, for ever and ever. Amen.

MONDAY
A Place to Live

Jesus answered . . . "Whoever loves me will keep my word, and my Father will love him, and we will come to him and make our dwelling with him. Whoever does not love me does not keep my words" (John 14:23-24).

Reflection: Everyone needs a place to live. Some people live in luxurious mansions with acres of manicured lawns and enormous swimming pools. Some people live in homes with enough space for the gathering of family members as well as sufficient private rooms to meet individual needs. Other people are forced to live in shacks or under bridges or on the street. Wherever people live, they must be comfortable living with themselves. A fine house or a street corner does not make a dwelling place for the individual spirit. If the individual spirit is not at home, then the person has not yet found a home.

Reaction: Is your dwelling place a home where your spirit is also at home?

Prayer: God of love, you have promised to make your home in the hearts of all who believe in you. Enable us to love Jesus and to keep his word. We ask you to come with Jesus and the Spirit and dwell in us that we might find rest and be one with you, who live and reign as one God, for ever and ever. Amen.

TUESDAY
Peace

"Peace I leave with you; my peace I give to you. Not as the world gives do I give it to you. Do not let your hearts be troubled or afraid" (John 14:27).

Reflection: Is peace the absence of war? Is peace a state of calm or quiet? Is peace mere obedience to laws? Is peace the reconciliation of strained relationships? Is peace a relationship that fosters friendship? Is peace death? Is peace a gift to be shared? Is it that feeling that comes over people when others alleviate their troubles and fears? Is it something that can be gained from the world?

Reaction: Formulate your definition of peace.

Prayer: God of peace, from our hearts you remove our troubles and erase our fears and leave us with your gift of peace. During this Easter Season we celebrate the peace accomplished by the death and Resurrection of Jesus. One day may we experience the fullness of his peace greeting and share the joys of the kingdom, where you live and reign with him and the Holy Spirit, one God, for ever and ever. Amen.

WEDNESDAY
Closeness

"Remain in me, as I [Jesus] remain in you. Just as a branch cannot bear fruit on its own unless it remains on the vine, so neither can you unless you remain in me. I am the vine, you are the branches. Whoever remains in me and I in him will bear much fruit" (John 15:4-5).

Reflection: Most people know how important it is to remain close to family, friends, a social group, a study group, a church, a business, whatever. Those who are on intimate terms with others remain actively engaged in the project at hand. Such persons — by interacting with others — begin to grow and at the same time aid in the growth of others. Much fruit is produced through such closeness. However, persons who isolate themselves may be taking years off their lives. Those who refuse this closeness to others cut themselves off from the flow of life.

Reaction: Name some people with whom you are close. How does each person enhance your life? How do you enhance their lives?

Prayer: God of life, all that exists comes through the power of your creative word. By your will we are brought to birth in the human family. Through your care you sustain our lives. Never let us be separated from you. Make all people fruitful brother-

and-sister branches united to Jesus, the vine. We ask this through our Lord Jesus Christ, your Son, who lives and reigns with you and the Holy Spirit, one God, for ever and ever. Amen.

THURSDAY
Comparisons

"As the Father loves me, so I also love you. Remain in my love. If you keep my commandments, you will remain in my love, just as I have kept my Father's commandments and remain in his love. I have told you this so that my joy might be in you and your joy might be complete" (John 15:9-11).

Reflection: In order to explain something that is not understood, people frequently make use of comparisons. When, for example, they try to tell another what a certain fruit tastes like, they will inevitably state that it tastes like something else. Or, in other areas, they will say, "That is as hard as wood." "This is as cold as ice." "That is as hot as fire." Teachers spend most of their time in class leading students from what is unknown to what is known by way of comparisons. When the unknown finally becomes known through the medium of comparison, then the joy of both teachers and learners is complete.

Reaction: To what do you compare love? Make a list of as many comparisons as possible.

Prayer: God of joy, you have revealed your great love for your people through comparisons: Jesus of Nazareth is the bread of life, the light of the world, the Good Shepherd, and the vine. Make our joy complete by enabling us to remain in the same love that you share with him and that he shares with you in the unity of your Holy Spirit, one God, for ever and ever. Amen.

FRIDAY
Friends

"This is my commandment: love one another as I love you. No one has greater love than this, to lay down one's life for one's friends. You are my friends if you do what I command you" (John 15:12-14).

Reflection: There are degrees of difference between acquaintances and friends. An acquaintance may be a person one has met at a social function or perhaps a person with whom one has done business. The name as well as a few other facts may be known about an acquaintance. However, the person is not known. A friend is one who is willing to know another person and to be known by the other person. Friends share a degree of closeness wherein both joy and pain, love and hate, strengths and weaknesses can be revealed to each other. A friend is willing to sacrifice time, money, effort — yes, even life — to foster the friendship because the relationship is life-giving.

Acquaintances are often forgotten; friends are remembered forever.

Reaction: Is Jesus your friend or just an acquaintance?

Prayer: Friendly God, you have never ceased to call every person to a relationship with you. Even when people refused your offer, you sought them out in the person of Jesus. He called his disciples to be his friends. He demonstrated his love for all people — his friends — by offering his life on the Cross. Give us the will to love each other as friends just as you love Jesus and he loves you in the unity of the love of the Holy Spirit, one God, for ever and ever. Amen.

SATURDAY
Hatred

"If the world hates you, realize that it hated me first. If you belonged to the world, the world would love its own; but because you do not belong to the world, and I have chosen you out of the world, the world hates you" (John 15:18-19).

Reflection: It is a tragic experience to hate or to be hated by another person. Hate makes its presence known in different ways. It can appear as apartheid in South Africa, segregation in the United States, or war in Iran. Hate destroys both the hater

66

and the hated. It destroys those who hate because such persons consume all of their energy in wreaking violence on another. It destroys those who are hated because of the intense feelings of retaliation that overwhelm them. When people hate each other, there is no winner; both the hater and the hated become losers.

Reaction: Have you ever hated or been hated by another person? What happened to you as a result of this experience?

Prayer: God of love, you have taught your people to reverence all life and to embrace each other as brothers and sisters. Through the sign of his Cross, Jesus, your Son, has overcome all division and prompted us to live a new life. When the hate of the world threatens to overcome us, make us realize that we no longer belong to this world but to the one of eternal life, where you live and reign with Jesus and the Holy Spirit, one God, for ever and ever. Amen.

SIXTH SUNDAY OF EASTER

Cycle A
Our Advocate

"I will ask the Father, and he will give you another Advocate to be with you always, the Spirit of truth, which the world cannot accept, because it neither sees nor knows it. But you know it, because it remains with you, and will be in you. I will not leave you orphans; I will come to you" (John 14:16-18).

Reflection: Advocates (paracletes) plead the cause of others. They act as defense attorneys; they intercede for others. One child is the advocate for another when asking, "Can John come out and play?" One friend speaks for another when she declares that "Jane could never have said or done that!" In a courtroom, a defense attorney states, "I will prove that my client is innocent of the crime with which he is accused." The purpose of an advocate is to speak the truth. An advocate ensures that another person is not left an orphan. The advocate comes to intercede for the orphan.

Reaction: Have others been advocates for you? How did they fulfill their function?

Prayer: God of the orphaned, you never abandon your people even when they turn away from you. With a father's love you seek them out. With a mother's open arms you welcome them back to you. Send us the Advocate promised by Jesus, the Spirit of truth, who loves and comforts and consoles us. We ask this through Jesus Christ, our Lord, who lives and reigns with you and the Holy Spirit, one God, for ever and ever. Amen.

Cycle B
Chosen Ones

"It was not you who chose me, but I who chose you and appointed you to go and bear fruit that will remain, so that whatever you ask the Father in my name he may give you. This I command you: love one another" (John 15:16-17).

Reflection: Most people have a variety of experiences in the area of choice — whether they are choosing or being chosen. When parents adopt, the child is chosen from all the other children. Most people remember the first time that they were chosen to be a member of a team. People are chosen for positions at their places of employment. In the world of sports, there are first draft choices. Throughout their lives people are chosen for a host of reasons. Whenever people are chosen, however, they are expected to produce. A child must grow into a man or a woman. A member of a team must play for the good of the whole team. At work, quality production is required of the one chosen. Those who are chosen for something are expected to bear fruit.

Reaction: When was the last time that you were chosen? What were you chosen for? Did you produce?

Prayer: God of the chosen, long ago you made the Israelites your Chosen People. You planted them like a vine in the Promised Land. From these people you chose the Virgin Mary to be the Mother of your only Son, Jesus Christ. He chose disciples to continue his work of spreading the Good News. Through the waters of Baptism you have chosen us to be your people, to praise your name and to serve you. Enable us to bear fruit. We ask this through our Lord Jesus Christ, your Son, who lives and reigns with you and the Holy Spirit, one God, for ever and ever. Amen.

Cycle C
Saying Good-bye

"You heard me tell you, 'I am going away and I will come back to you.' If you loved me, you would rejoice that I am going to the Father; for the Father is greater than I" (John 14:28).

Reflection: Saying "Good-bye" to someone who is loved is difficult to do; it ushers in a long-term separation. And yet good-byes are an important part of life. After the birth of a child, the parents must say good-bye the first night they leave the child with a sitter. Children say good-bye to their parents on the first day of school. Friends say good-bye as they move to a different part of the country. All must say a final good-bye to the world at the time of death. Sad good-byes must eventually follow joyous hellos. But since those who leave may eventually return, a present good-bye may become a future hello.

Reaction: Recall the times you have had to say good-bye to those whom you loved. Have you had the opportunity to say hello to them in a new way? How?

Prayer: God of love, your people continue through the years to bid you good-bye, but you refuse to let them go. Your Son, Jesus, as he hung on the Cross, declared that he thought that you had abandoned him. However, you greeted him with the hello of Resurrection. Ignore our moments of good-bye and greet us with a heavenly hello. Help us to discover the new life that awaits us where you live and reign with Jesus Christ, our Lord, and the Holy Spirit, one God, for ever and ever. Amen.

MONDAY
Free Information

"When the Advocate comes whom I will send you from the Father, the Spirit of truth that proceeds from the Father, he will testify to me. And you also testify, because you have been with me from the beginning. . . . I have told you this so that when their hour comes you may remember that I told you" (John 15:26-27; 16:4).

Reflection: When people share facts with others, free information is being passed between them. "You have a flat tire on your car" is free information. "Did you realize that the meeting for next week has been canceled?" is free information. "Your shoe is untied" is free information. These exchanges take place throughout each day. Those who give the information presume that the person receiving it will do something about it. They expect that the flat tire will be fixed, that the change of the meeting date will be duly noted, and that the shoelace will be tied. If information is really free, it cannot be used by another for manipulation. Once it is given, the giver abandons it. All a person can do is to hope that the one who receives it will remember it at the appropriate time.

Reaction: When was the last time someone gave you some free information? Did you act on it or ignore it?

Prayer: God of free information, you have never ceased to communicate with your people. You spoke to your patriarchs, who followed your directions and led your people to the Promised Land. You spoke to your prophets, who proclaimed your word and urged your people to turn away from sin. You have spoken to us in Jesus, your Son, the Word-made-flesh. Give us hearts that are ready to listen to him, who can show us the way to you and the Spirit, who live and reign with him, one God, for ever and ever. Amen.

TUESDAY
Parting Gift

"I am going to the one who sent me, and not one of you asks me, 'Where are you going?' But because I told you this, grief has filled your hearts. But I tell you the truth, it is better for you that I go. For if I do not go, the Advocate will not come to you. But if I go, I will send him to you" (John 16:5-7).

Reflection: Gifts come in a variety of shapes and sizes. Some of them come wrapped in bright paper tied with ribbons and a bow. Some come through the mail in a brown-colored carton. Other gifts are certificates or tickets. Seldom, however, do people consider separating from another or going away from another to be a gift. There is more truth in the old saying that parting is such sweet sorrow than most people would like to admit. Parting from another can truly be a gift because it gives a personal space to each of the persons involved in the relationship. This time away from their loved ones enables people to deepen their appreciation for others, to grow in their individual personalities, and to look forward to the return of the loved one. Otherwise, standing in the presence of each other becomes routine and the possibility of taking each other for granted is ever present.

Reaction: When was the last time that parting from a loved one was a gift for you?

Prayer: God of truth, you sent your Son, Jesus, into the world to teach your people the mystery of suffering and death. When he had parted from us in death, you returned him to us through the power of his Resurrection. Send into our lives the Advocate, the giver of life. Grant that when we leave this world in death we may share in the Resurrection of Jesus, who lives and reigns with you and the Holy Spirit, one God, for ever and ever. Amen.

WEDNESDAY
Saying Hello Again

"It is better for you that I go. For if I do not go, the Advocate will not come to you. But if I go, I will send him to you. . . . When he comes, the Spirit of truth, he will guide you to all truth" (John 16:7,13).

Reflection: Every person knows how difficult it is to say good-bye to a member of the family or a close friend when that person is permanently leaving home, leaving the city, or embarking on a lengthy journey. It is even more difficult to say good-bye if the context is death. But unless the good-bye is voiced and the departure begun, there is no opportunity to say hello to new family, new friends, or to welcome someone home. When it comes to relinquishing what was believed to be the truth in favor of newly discovered truth, the pain of separation from old ideas, old practices, and old conceptions is felt. The promise inherent in every old good-bye is that there will be a new hello. What is so strange in all of this is that the new hello is like being baptized with the spirit of the old good-bye.

Reaction: What newness did you find in your life the last time that you said "hello again"?

Prayer: God of promises, you have faithfully kept the old covenant that you made with your people in the past. In the blood of Jesus, your Son, you established a new covenant. Through his death, Resurrection, and gift of the Spirit, he has enabled us to share in his fullness of resurrected life. Guide us as fathers and mothers direct the steps of their children. Protect us as an elder brother who rallies his brothers and sisters around him. And seal us with the Paraclete, the promised gift. We ask this through Jesus Christ, your Son, who with you and the Holy Spirit are one God, for ever and ever. Amen.

THURSDAY

SOLEMNITY OF THE ASCENSION
Cycle A
Living the Good News

The eleven disciples went to Galilee, to the mountain to which Jesus had ordered them. When they saw him, they worshiped, but they doubted. Then Jesus approached and said to them, "All power in heaven and on earth has been given to me. Go, therefore, and make disciples of all nations, baptizing them in the name of the Father, and of the Son, and of the holy Spirit, teaching them to observe all that I have commanded you. And behold, I am with you always, until the end of the age" (Matthew 28:16-20).

Reflection: Through Baptism all people have been given authority and the corresponding responsibility to "make disciples of all nations." This is not a recipe-oriented task; rather, its effectiveness depends on the way Christians live their lives. Lifestyle is the best evangelizer because it teaches others the priorities of a follower of Jesus. It baptizes them with a message that is better heard than any delivered in pulpits, on television, or over public address systems. The strength to adhere to a particular lifestyle that characterizes a follower of Jesus is given by Jesus himself. He has not abandoned his followers; he is with them always. When they live as he lived, when they evangelize as he evangelized, when they teach as he taught, it is he doing all this through them. He is with them until the end.

Reaction: In what way does your lifestyle illustrate that you are a follower of Jesus?

Prayer: God of the infinite, you gave us Jesus as an example of how to live. He traveled our land, taught our people, lived our way of life, and invited us to follow him. Enable us to practice his way. Help us to know his presence which stretches throughout eternity, where he is Lord with you and the Holy Spirit, one God, for ever and ever. Amen.

Cycle B
Proclaiming the Gospel

He [Jesus] said to them "Go into the whole world and proclaim the gospel to every creature. . . . " Then the Lord Jesus, after he spoke to them, was taken up into heaven and took his seat at the right hand of God (Mark 16:15,19).

Reflection: The proclamation of messages takes place everywhere in our world. The radio proclaims. The television proclaims. The newspapers proclaim. Perhaps because there is so much proclamation, most people never hear the message. But there is another kind of proclamation which is seldom used: the personal approach. People share with others the active presence of God in their lives. Such witness to the Gospel message does not even need words. Reverence for birds, squirrels, and rabbits proclaims good news. Care for the resources of the earth is a proclamation of the Gospel. And recognition of the human dignity of all people delivers a message of good news to the whole world. Many times the best message is delivered without words.

Reaction: How often have you delivered a good news message without saying a single word?

Prayer: God of good news, after people had sinned and turned away from you, you proclaimed the good news of forgiveness. Jesus, your Son, came into the world and proclaimed the Gospel in word and deed. His death on the Cross spoke eloquently of your love for us. However, in raising him from the dead you proclaimed the message of eternal life. Enable us to be bearers of the Good News in our words and our actions, so that we may share in the eternal life of Jesus, who lives and reigns with you and the Holy Spirit, one God, for ever and ever. Amen.

Cycle C
Confronting Abandonment

Then he [Jesus] led them out as far as Bethany, raised his hands, and blessed them. As he blessed them he parted from them and was taken up to heaven. They did him homage and then returned to Jerusalem with great joy (Luke 24:50-52).

Reflection: Abandonment is a terrifying feeling of being alone. No one cares. No one is around. People experience abandonment in divorce, in death, in good-byes, in sickness. When a person suffers loneliness, there is a temptation to lose all hope. Sooner or later, however, such a one must rise up and return to living. Everyone must recognize that abandonment is part and parcel of being human, of being alive; and it is good because it is redemptive.

Life's traveling companions sometimes abandon their fellow pilgrims. But this should not cause the other pilgrims to falter. In order to share in any new dimension of life, most of the old has to be abandoned and set free. Those who practice this kind of abandonment stand with arms upraised in prayer and hands open to receive (or to have what is in them removed) at the will of the One who raised Jesus from the dead.

Reaction: Have you ever felt abandoned by others? Did you find the presence of God in this abandonment?

Prayer: God of abandonment, you did not forget the broken body of your Son on the Cross. Once he had abandoned his life into your hands, you raised him up to the fullness of eternal life. Instill in us his vision. Let us know your presence with us in the times when we feel abandoned. We hope too, that some day you will take us to heaven where you live with your Son and your Holy Spirit as one God, for ever and ever. Amen.

THURSDAY
*(In places where the celebration
of Ascension is transferred
to the Seventh Sunday of Easter)*
Gone Astray

"A little while and you will no longer see me, and again a little while later and you will see me" (John 16:16).

Reflection: It is very easy to get lost these days. A person can get lost on the road and drive for miles in the wrong direction. Another person can get lost in a building searching for an office on the wrong floor. Some people get lost in their beliefs and no longer see the direction their faith is leading them. However, no matter how people get lost, ultimately they can find their way. Once the wrong road direction is discovered, the right course can be taken. Once the correct floor number is detected, the office can be found. And once faith is reawakened, a person's response indicates a new direction.

Reaction: When was the last time that you were lost? What did you learn from the experience?

Prayer: God of the lost, you seek each person as a shepherd patrols the pasture for the sheep that has strayed. When we are lost in our journey of faith, come and find us and lead us home to where you live with Jesus Christ, our Lord, and the Holy Spirit, one God, for ever and ever. Amen.

FRIDAY
Accepting Pain

"When a woman is in labor, she is in anguish because her hour has arrived; but when she has given birth to a child, she no longer remembers the pain because of her joy that a child has been born into the world. So you also are now in anguish. But I will see you again, and your hearts will rejoice, and no one will take your joy away from you" (John 16:21-22).

Reflection: Life is difficult. Authentic living is filled with pain. Many people can't stand the pain and attempt to avoid it. The drugstore is filled with over-the-counter products that are guaranteed to eliminate the pain from living. However, drugging pain removes one of the characteristics of being human. Pain derives from our human condition. Once we have experienced it, we are able to sympathize with others when they are feeling it. If a person embraces pain as part of the human experience instead of attempting to avoid or ignore it, that person knows the joy that waits on the other side of it. It is like the joy of a mother that follows the pain of giving birth to a child.

Reaction: After you have embraced pain, have you ever discovered a kind of joy that no one could take from you?

Prayer: God our healer, you did not remove the pain of suffering and death from your Son, Jesus. Rather, you strengthened him so that he could embrace the pain of the Cross, and then you

gave him the joy of the Resurrection. In him you have given us
an example. Strengthen us in our suffering and enable us to give
birth to new life. May we one day be joyful in your presence,
where you are one God, Father, Son, and Holy Spirit, for ever
and ever. Amen.

SATURDAY
Obtaining Insurance

**"Amen, amen, I say to you, whatever you ask the Father
in my name he will give you. Until now you have not asked
anything in my name; ask and you will receive, so that
your joy may be complete" (John 16:23-24).**

Reflection: Most people pay for some kind of insurance which
functions as a protection for them. There is car insurance, which
protects people from the cost of an accident and the cost of
repairs to a car. There is health insurance, which protects them
from the cost of hospitalization. There is home insurance,
which protects them from fire, theft, or natural disasters. All of
these kinds of insurance promise to protect the buyer from
excessive financial burdens. Once in a while a person will offer
"asking" insurance. "Whatever you ask, I will do for you."
"If you need something, give me a call." "If I can help in any
way, let me know." "Asking" insurance is based on trust that
the request, which will make the requester happy, will be
granted.

Reaction: Has anyone ever offered you "asking" insurance? Who was this? Did you make use of it?

Prayer: God of mercy, you have assured us that whatever we ask for will be given to us. Strengthen our trust in your promise and enable us to make petition in your name. Make our joy complete with the new life of Jesus, who lives and reigns with you and the Holy Spirit, one God, for ever and ever. Amen.

SEVENTH SUNDAY OF EASTER

Cycle A
The Hour

"He [Jesus] raised his eyes to heaven and said, 'Father, the hour has come. Give glory to your son, so that your son may glorify you, just as you gave him authority over all people, so that he may give eternal life to all you gave him' " (John 17:1-2).

Reflection: The hour comes for everyone. There is a time in all people's lives when they must make a decision and live with the consequences. There comes a time in every person's life when one thing has to be given up in order to possess another thing. There is a time in all people's lives when they must confront the finality of death. The hour is different for everyone; but, whatever the hour, it comes for each person. Instead of running away from the hour, it is better to face it. Once it is faced, once the decision is made, once something is relinquished, once death is confronted, then the person can enjoy the glory that results from such an encounter.

Reaction: What "hour" have you had to face lately? Once you faced it, did you find any glory?

Prayer: God of the hour, throughout the years and days and hours of life, you watch over your people. At the right hour during the night you led your Chosen People from slavery to freedom and helped them to defeat their enemies; they gave glory to you. On the Cross, your Son glorified your name. You bestowed upon him the glory of the Resurrection. May we come to share in eternal life, where you, the one God, are glorified with Jesus Christ, our Lord, and your Holy Spirit, for ever and ever. Amen.

Cycle B
Fatherly Protection

"Holy Father, keep them in your name that you have given me, so that they may be one just as we are. When I was with them I protected them in your name that you gave me, and I guarded them" (John 17:11-12).

Reflection: Protection creates a secure feeling. Parents protect and guard their children. Homeowners and business managers enjoy the protection offered by their security systems; they are guarded from theft. Safety belts in automobiles provide protection for riders. A name can also protect and guard. People do this by making sure that they project a good image to others in their neighborhood and to the media. They associate with the right people and are careful to be seen doing all the right things. Such protection creates security.

Reaction: Do you use your name for protection as described here?

Prayer: God of protection, you have guarded your people as an eagle guards her young. When slavery threatened the freedom of your people, you released them from Pharaoh's chains. When hunger and thirst threatened their existence, you gave them food and drink. As a mother who gathers her chicks under her wings, gather us under your name. Watch over us and protect us always. We ask this through our Lord Jesus Christ, your Son, who lives and reigns with you and the Holy Spirit, one God, for ever and ever. Amen.

Cycle C
Seeking Unity

"I [Jesus] pray . . . that they [those who believe] may all be one, as you, Father, are in me and I in you, that they also may be in us, that the world may believe that you sent me. And I have given them the glory you gave me, so that they may be one, as we are one, I in them and you in me, that they may be brought to perfection as one, that the world may know that you sent me, and that you loved them even as you loved me. Father, they are your gift to me. I wish that where I am they also may be with me, that

they may see my glory that you gave me, because you loved me before the foundation of the world" (John 17:20-24).

Reflection: People habitually strive for unity among themselves. A party is declared to be a success if all those invited had a good time interacting with each other. Success is attributed to a team if all the members form a unity so that whatever is done is for the good of the team. Family reunions are held to emphasize the unity of the many members of the family. Committee members seek unity to make their task easier. And week after week members of congregations gather at Mass to break bread with each other in order to make visible their unity. This longing for unity with others reveals in its fullness the human dimension of all people.

Reaction: Make a list of the various groups of people with whom you meet. What was the last activity that each engaged in to display its unity?

Prayer: God of unity, in you there is found no division. In perfect love you are one God in three persons. Come and dwell in us as the Father dwells in Jesus and Jesus dwells in the Father. Abide in us as both are in the Spirit as the Spirit is in both of them. May we be one as you are one. We ask this through our Lord Jesus Christ, your Son, who lives and reigns with you and the Holy Spirit, one God, for ever and ever. Amen.

MONDAY
Talking Plainly

His disciples said, "Now you are talking plainly, and not in any figure of speech. Now we realize that you know everything and that you do not need to have anyone question you. Because of this we believe that you came from God." Jesus answered them, "Do you believe now?" (John 16:29-31)

Reflection: The quickest way to get anyone to believe or understand anything is to speak plainly to that person. Many times people say, "Put that in language that I understand." "I don't know what you're talking about." "Translate that for me." These statements reveal that what was spoken was too complicated. When people understand, they do not ask for much clarification. Plain language is the best way to convince others. Of course, once someone professes belief or understanding, it might be wise to ask, "Do you really understand or believe?" At times people think they understand when in fact they don't. Some people practice believing for so many years that they are not sure whether they believe or whether they are still just practicing to believe.

Reaction: Do you really believe in Jesus? State your beliefs in plain language.

Prayer: God of all believers, you have spoken plainly throughout time so that people might believe in you. Jesus, your Son, spoke plainly of your love for us. As we profess our belief in the mystery of your Godhead, strengthen our weak faith. We ask this through our Lord Jesus Christ, who lives and reigns with you and the Holy Spirit, one God, for ever and ever. Amen.

TUESDAY
Life's Parentheses

"This is eternal life, that they should know you, the only true God, and the one whom you sent, Jesus Christ" (John 17:3).

Reflection: In some editions of the Bible the verse above is printed in parentheses to indicate that it explains the phrase "eternal life," which occurs in the preceding verse. These marks indicate that the remark or sentence amplifies the theme of a discourse. More often than not, most of what people speak is parenthetical. They state a simple fact and then proceed to use hundreds of words to give examples, defend, and clarify the statement. In fact, most of life is parenthetical. Little newness is ever added to the daily pattern; only nuancing takes place.

Reaction: In the past year, what changes have you made in your daily routine of living?

Prayer: God of life, when you created people in your image and likeness, you gave them the breath of life. When Jesus, your

Son, slept in the tomb, you filled him with the breath of eternal life. We have come to know you, the only true God, and Jesus, the One whom you have sent. Send your Spirit into the routine of our lives and fill us with the breath of the Resurrection. We ask this through our Lord Jesus Christ, your Son, who lives and reigns with you and the Holy Spirit, one God, for ever and ever. Amen.

WEDNESDAY
Belonging

"I [Jesus] gave them [the disciples] your word, and the world hated them, because they do not belong to the world any more than I belong to the world. I do not ask that you take them out of the world but that you keep them from the evil one" (John 17:14-15).

Reflection: Most people live where they belong. Since people experience themselves living in the world, they logically belong to the world. How, then, can one live in the world and not belong to the world? Certainly, one cannot live outside of the world or be taken out of the world except by death. Attitudinally, a person can live in the world and not belong to it. Such a person is not interested in fashion, money, recognition, whatever. These types of persons may be called odd or strange, and they are despised and hated and ostracized for not belonging to the same world as everyone else. Sometimes, these persons are also called saints.

Reaction: Do you live in the world and yet not belong to it?

Prayer: God of all nations, in countless ways throughout the ages you have issued your call to all people to hear your word and to live according to your commands. Jesus, your Son, called men and women to be his disciples; he instructed them to live in the world but not to belong to it. Give us the spirit of discernment that we might respond to your word and follow Jesus unreservedly, for he lives and reigns with you and the Holy Spirit, one God, for ever and ever. Amen.

THURSDAY
Knowing

"Righteous Father, the world also does not know you, but I know you, and they know that you sent me. I made known to them your name and I will make it known, that the love with which you loved me may be in them and I in them" (John 17:25-26).

Reflection: Many people associate knowing with knowledge. If people don't know a certain thing, they have not learned it; they have no knowledge of it. If they do know a certain thing, then they have learned it; they have knowledge of it. This kind of knowledge is like knowing a person's name. However, there is another type of knowledge which goes beyond knowing about something or having the right information. This other kind of knowledge is centered on a person. One not only knows a person's name but also knows the unique, inner reality of the individual. Surface knowledge is safe; it requires no involvement of the one who declares knowledge or lack of knowledge on the subject. Inner knowledge involves a risk of getting involved just like love does.

Reaction: How many people do you really know? How many people really know you?

Prayer: Righteous God, you called your Chosen People by name and invited them to risk a relationship with you. In Baptism you have named us and promised to reveal yourself to us throughout our life's journey. May our love for you deepen and grow. We ask this through our Lord Jesus Christ, your Son, who lives and reigns with you and the Holy Spirit, one God, for ever and ever. Amen.

FRIDAY
Growing Old

"Amen, amen, I say to you [Peter], when you were younger, you used to dress yourself and go where you wanted; but when you grow old, you will stretch out your hands, and someone else will dress you and lead you where you do not want to go." He said this signifying by what kind of death he would glorify God. And when he had said this, he said to him, "Follow me" (John 21:18-19).

Reflection: Many people fear growing old because they will no longer be in control of their lives. After dressing themselves, cooking for themselves, driving themselves, keeping house for themselves, and working on their own for decades, they suddenly find that they are no longer able to maintain these activities and must depend upon others to do these things for them. For some people this means living with relatives or friends or moving into a nursing home. More often than not, a lot of suffering is involved in the move because those who are old do not want to relinquish control of their lives.

Reaction: What is your greatest fear about growing old?

Prayer: Eternal God, you are changeless and timeless. You bring us to birth. You nourish us with your word. You guide our feet on the right paths. And when our days are numbered, you call us home to yourself. Through his death, Jesus has shown us the way to you. Give us a share in his Resurrection. Grant this through the same Jesus Christ, our Lord, who lives and reigns with you and the Holy Spirit, one God, for ever and ever. Amen.

SATURDAY
Our Life Stories

There are also many other things that Jesus did, but if these were to be described individually, I do not think the whole world would contain the books that would be written (John 21:25).

Reflection: The deeds of Jesus continue to be written. In journals people record their reflections, which are the deeds of Jesus in their lives. In books, theologians, Scripture scholars, and other learned people attempt to organize and analyze the unusual activity of Jesus that continues today. And other people write with their lives; their actions in soup kitchens, in health care centers, in shelters, wherever, proclaim the deeds of Jesus. The whole world could not contain all the books that would have to be written if all people recorded what Jesus has done and is doing for them.

Reaction: What is Jesus doing in your life?

Prayer: God of the written word, through parchment and ink and paper and print you have delivered your message of love to your people. No book or printed word can capture the whole of your revelation. So you write with the lives of your faithful people. As we read this word, give us understanding. Help us to know you and the one whom you sent, Jesus Christ, who lives and reigns with you and the Holy Spirit, one God, for ever and ever. Amen.

SOLEMNITY OF PENTECOST

Cycles A, B, and C
Filled With the Spirit

When the time for Pentecost was fulfilled, they [the disciples] were all in one place together. And suddenly there came from the sky a noise like a strong driving wind, and it filled the entire house in which they were. Then there appeared to them tongues as of fire, which parted and came to rest on each one of them. And they were all filled with the holy Spirit and began to speak in different tongues, as the Spirit enabled them to proclaim (Acts 2:1-4).

Reflection: All people have experienced Pentecost. They have had some strong, driving force in their lives that pushed them in the right direction. This could have been a concerned parent, a trusted friend, or a business associate. The push was so powerful that others heard about it or witnessed the new spirit that motivated these people to do things they formerly thought impossible. It was as if these persons were on fire! Incidents abound of those who break out of their quiet shells and begin to speak with the kind of wisdom which even they did not think possible. They are filled with the spirit of new life.

Reaction: When were you last filled with the Spirit? Who was the strong, driving force for you?

Prayer: God of wind and fire, once, when your spirit hovered over the waters, you breathed life into your image, which you had formed from the dust of the earth. Send a strong, driving force into our lives today. Move us with a fire of urgency that speaks your Word. May the Spirit of your promise give birth in us to the resurrected life of Jesus, your Son, who with you and the Holy Spirit, live and reign as one God, for ever and ever. Amen.

Books for Other Church Seasons

DAY BY DAY THROUGH ADVENT
Reflections, Prayers, Practices

Based on the biblical reading for each day, this book presents a thoughtful reflection, offers a simple prayer, and suggests a helpful practice intended to open the heart and mind to the coming of Jesus. **$2.25**

OUR HEARTS WAIT
Daily Prayer for Advent

A few lines from the Gospel reading become the basis for a daily reflection, followed by a practical way to extend the reflection into daily life. **$1.50**

ADVENT BEGINS AT HOME
Family Prayers and Activities

Prayers and activities to make Advent a time of sharing and preparing for a Christ-centered Christmas. **$1.95**

DAY BY DAY THROUGH LENT
Reflections, Prayers, Practices

A practical way to "keep" Lent by applying the Word of God to daily life. A thought, prayer, and idea for each day helps you grow in understanding and love. **$3.95**

A LENTEN JOURNEY WITH JESUS
Prayerful Steps for Each Day

An invitation to take forty "inward" steps based on the Gospel of the day. Includes a simple, yet helpful, "prayer focus" for each day. **$1.50**

LENT BEGINS AT HOME
Family Prayers and Activities

This positive approach to Lent includes ideas for prayer, discussion, and projects that the family can do together. **$1.50**

LENT IS FOR CHILDREN
Stories, Activities, Prayers

Written for children in the middle-elementary grades, this book presents suggested practices and activities to reinforce Lenten basics. **$1.95**

Order from your local bookstore or write to:
Liguori Publications, Box 060, Liguori, Missouri 63057
*(Please add 75¢ for postage and handling for
first item ordered and 25¢ for each additional item.)*